Contents

What is a cartoon?

I love cartoons. They're fun to watch, read and draw. The best cartoons make me laugh out loud, whether they are quick sketches drawn with a pencil, or a feature-length animated movie. They also inspire me to draw my own. It's not hard, once you've mastered a few simple tricks. This book has loads of great ideas!

Having a laugh!

Cartoons are a great way to explore the funny side of life. Most cartoons focus on an invented character or characters. They make us smile by simplifying or exaggerating one or two key features such as eyes or hands. While the drawing is unrealistic, we still recognise what it represents.

Matt Groening, creator of *The Simpsons*, has this advice for anyone who's starting out as a cartoonist: *"…Do what makes you laugh, don't try to make other people laugh…that's when you start writing from the heart, and then people will get it."*

THE EXPERT SAYS...

CHECKLIST

This is all you need to get started:

- ☑ paper
- ☑ pencil and pen
- ☑ sense of humour
- ☑ imagination

Tell a story

Some cartoons need no words at all. Others have words, known as captions, which complete the joke or add to the humour. A 'comic strip' is a series of drawings. When the drawings are viewed in sequence they tell a story. Comic books and graphic novels are longer versions of the comic strip. They tell detailed stories, sometimes with a large cast of characters.

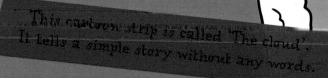

This cartoon strip is called 'The cloud'. It tells a simple story without any words.

Getting started

Spongebob Squarepants is a simple box shape with eyes, a mouth and little arms and legs.

Cartoons don't have to be complicated. Some of the best cartoons are drawn with a few simple lines. You can create a great cartoon character with a basic body shape like a blob or a square. I usually start by doodling with a pencil to find a shape I like, and then I add some eyes. Once the eyes are in place, I make it up as I go along!

THE EXPERT SAYS...

Ideas can come from anywhere! Spongebob Squarepants started life as Bob the Sponge. His creator, Stephen Hillenburg, had the idea for his famous cartoon character while working at a marine pool centre and teaching visitors about the animal life there.

Stick figures

If you want to draw people quickly or you find arms and legs tricky, try drawing stick figures. Start with a circle for a head. Next add a vertical line for the body, with two more joining it for the arms and two for the legs. You can then add eyes, a nose, a mouth, hair, stick hands or maybe a prop like a phone or an ice cream. But only if you want to!

All about the eyes

When you look at a cartoon character, what do you notice first? Often it's the eyes. Most of the eyes shown here have a basic round or half-moon shape with a dot or small circle inside. The position of the dot tells us WHERE the the character is looking. The shape of the eye tells us HOW they are looking. And the eyebrows definitely add some extra expression!

CHECKLIST

To design a cartoon monster:

- ✓ Draw a circle with a pencil
- ✓ Draw a cross through it
- ✓ Add some arm and leg lines
- ✓ Draw two eyes in the top half
- ✓ Add a mouth in the bottom half
- ✓ Build up any extra features like hair or hands – be as wacky as you like!
- ✓ Use a pen to ink the finished outline and rub out any pencil marks.

Try drawing some of these eye shapes yourself.

top tip

Some cartoons mix up things that don't normally go together. A shark wearing sunglasses? A basketball with a mouth? Use circles, ovals and rectangles to build the basic body shape, then add some accessories!

Looks familiar?

A cartoon can be completely unrealistic, yet everyone can see who, or what it is. I sometimes draw cartoon versions of myself. First, I decide which features I'm going to focus on. I have curly hair, quite a pointy chin and a really big smile, so when I've drawn a head shape I exaggerate those features. Then everyone knows it's me!

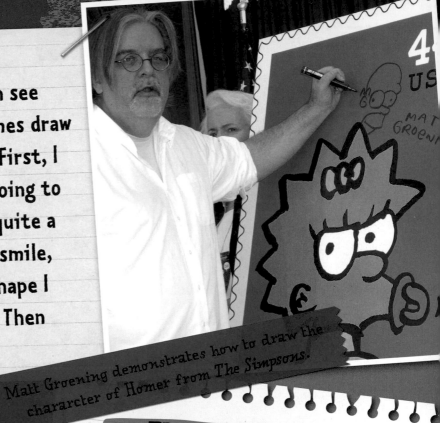

Matt Groening demonstrates how to draw the chararcter of Homer from The Simpsons.

Caricature

An exaggerated cartoon likeness of someone is called a caricature. Caricatures have been around for hundreds of years; some examples date from Ancient Rome. Sometimes they are used to mock or make fun of public figures such as celebrities or politicians, but most caricatures are drawn for everyone to enjoy. This includes the person being drawn; after all, we're pretty funny!

CHECKLIST

To create a recognisable caricature of someone you know, think about their:

- ☑ hairstyle
- ☑ any facial hair such as a beard
- ☑ accessories such as glasses, earrings, hats or scarves
- ☑ make-up

Capture the character

A caricature isn't just about exaggerating a person's most obvious features. A good caricaturist also tries to show a person's character. Now think about your friends or family members. What expressions do they use? For example, do they raise one eyebrow higher than the other? What props might give us clues about them?

Look at this cartoon drawing of a cartoonist. Apart from how he looks, we also learn something else about him. The clue is in the pencil!

DO IT YOURSELF

Sit in front of a mirror and think about the shape of your head. Is it pointed, or round, or square, or long? Try drawing your basic head shape, exaggerating its pointiness or roundness. Next pick two of your most obvious features, and exaggerate them in your drawing. Finally, add your other features, but keep them as simple and small as possible. Show it to your friends without telling them who it is. Do they recognise you?

top tip

The best person to practise on is you!

Comic strips

The Beano's most famous comic strip character is Dennis the Menace.

I'm a big fan of comic strips and comic books. I love the way they tell jokes and stories – you see what's going on and the humour is shown through the drawing. My favourite comic strips are the ones that use the same cast of characters each time. You get to know all their funny habits and problems!

Tell me a story

Comic strips tell a joke or a story in a series of pictures. They have been around for a long time. In Medieval times most people couldn't read, so pictures were a good way to share stories. The Bayeux Tapestry, showing the sequence of events at the Battle of Hastings, is a type of early comic strip! Nowadays the book-length comic format, or graphic novel, is becoming more and more popular.

A scene from the Bayeux Tapestry

Panels

A panel is a single picture, usually in a box, or frame. A comic strip is made up of a series of panels, drawn in sequence so that the reader knows which one to look at next. A short strip might use only three or four panels that move in a line from left to right. A longer strip might fill a whole page with panels of different shapes and sizes. When this happens, it's helpful if each panel is numbered.

Have a go at creating a three-panel comic strip to show someone struggling to open a door. In the first panel they try turning the handle. In the second panel they use a bit of force. What happens in the third panel? Will you use any words?

top tip

This cartoon from the nineteenth century used a lot of words!

USING WORDS

You don't have to use words in a comic strip or even in a graphic novel - sometimes the pictures are all you need. If you do want to include words, be brief!

Put speech in speech bubbles...

... and unspoken thoughts in thought bubbles.

Keep any explanations short and box them off separately.

Superheroes

I've started collecting superhero comics. *Spiderman* is my favourite. I love the way his special powers come from a spider's bite. He can spin webs, walk up walls and even hang upside down from the ceiling. Mind you, the villains are often the craziest characters. They always have strong personality traits, like The Joker in *Batman* who plays evil jokes on his enemies. They're the characters we love to hate!

Spiderman was created more than 50 years ago by Stan Lee and Steve Ditko

Action and suspense

Some comics use the panel form of storytelling to create long-running series full of action and suspense. These stories focus on super-powered heroes like Superman and Catwoman. Two American publishers, Marvel and DC Comics (left), are famous for their comic-book superheroes and, of course, the fiendish super-villains who want to take over the world!

Larger-than-life

Superheroes are hugely exaggerated. Their physical abilities are superhuman; they face extreme peril; even the colours in each panel are bright, bold and unrealistic.

They may be deadly serious, but they're still super fun!

top tip

Do you want to create a superhero or superheroine? Start by asking yourself these questions:

1. What's their special power?

2. What's their secret weakness?

3. Who is their arch-enemy?

The first issue of the *X-Men* comic

CHECKLIST

Producing a full-colour comic like the *X-Men* involves many separate jobs. Which would you choose?

- ☑ plotter (the person who works out the story)

- ☑ penciller (the person who sketches the outline pictures)

- ☑ inker (the person who inks in the final outlines)

- ☑ colourist (the person who colours them in)

- ☑ letterer (the person who writes in the words).

Manga and animé

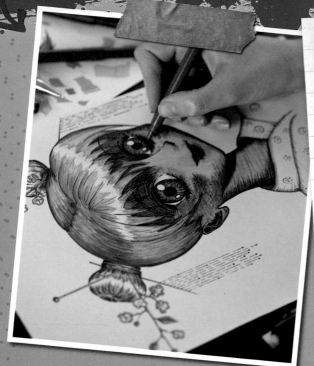

I love drawing manga-style cartoons. The characters have a really cool look with big eyes and lots of spiky hair and you can have so much fun with their costumes and their personalities. My friend Nita draws modern-day characters who wear baseball caps, jeans and trainers. I prefer creating fantasy costumes with flowing capes and dramatic headgear.

Cartoons from Japan

'Manga' means 'cartoon' in Japan, and animé is the animated version of manga. Manga comics are usually in black and white and stories are not limited to the action-adventure type, though this is popular. There are manga romances, manga historical stories, fantasy stories and stories about animals. A typical manga has complex, distinctive characters and a strong storyline. In Japan, everyone reads them — young and old alike.

Ken Sugimori made his name as the character designer and art director for the Pokémon cartoon brand and drew all of the original 151 Pokémon himself. He says he finds much of his inspiration by carefully observing animals in aquariums and zoos. He draws each character many times, making changes until he is satisfied with how it looks.

A certain style

Over the past 100 years or so, Japanese manga developed a distinctive style that has now become recognisable all over the world. As well as hugely exaggerated eyes and lots of hair, manga cartoons use speech bubbles in dramatic shapes, lines to suggest speed and movement, and lots of exclamation marks! Many manga cartoons have been made into serialised, full-colour animé.

Pokémon are colourful little monster characters, such as Pikachu, shown here, who are captured and trained by different Pokémon trainers.

top tip

To achieve that manga style yourself, use a black felt-tip to ink in the hair and the pupil of the eye but always leave a small, wedge-shaped area un-inked. This suggests reflected light and helps create the distinctive ultra-shiny look of the eyes and hair.

Create a comic

Me and my friends made a comic which we printed and handed out at school. We called it 'Comikatz!' Each of us created our own one-page comic strip with different cat characters. Mine was a manga-style cat called Super Shu. We all helped design the front page with the title. Then we photocopied each page and stapled them together. It looks pretty good!

The big picture

Making a comic with a variety of comic strips is a fun thing to do. One of the first decisions you'll make is what to call it. You might want all the cartoons to follow a theme such as wacky humour or fantasy adventure. You might want each cartoon to be drawn in the same style such as superhero, manga or stick drawing. Or you might aim for loads of variety! Try to choose a name that says something about the kind of comic it is.

PHOTOCOPYING

Will you photocopy your comic to give to family and friends? If you decide to print in black and white then make sure you draw in black and white, because some colours will look the same and you'll lose some of the detail when it prints out.

Plan your panels

When you have jotted down a story outline for each comic strip, work out how many panels you'll need and draw them lightly in pencil first. Then any mistakes can be rubbed out. And remember, not every panel needs to be the same size. If you have a particularly exciting scene you can make it really big, with smaller panels around it. Use numbers if the sequence gets confusing, and always save a big joke or surprise for the final one.

Outlining drawings before colouring

THE EXPERT SAYS...

Sarah McKintyre, cartoonist and comic book author, says: *"Comics are all about doing and making. If you don't know how to draw something, you write it; if you can't write it, you draw."* Alternatively, if drawing isn't your strong point, take pictures of toys or people acting out the scene, print them out, arrange them in the right sequence and stick speech bubbles on top.

Sarah McKintyre (right) gives the Duchess of Cornwall a lesson in how to draw cartoons.

Animation

Viewers look through the slits of this zoetrope as it spins, to see the horse move.

Animated cartoons are brilliant. They're funny, with colourful characters you don't forget in a hurry! They're also really clever. It can take weeks to make a few minutes of a well-known TV cartoon like *The Simpsons*, but animations don't have to be complicated. I've learned some great skills by making flipbooks.

Moving pictures

An animated cartoon is a series of linked images, often drawings, shown in rapid sequence so that the images appear to be moving. Before the invention of cameras, animation relied on mechanical tricks such as a zoetrope, a spinning drum with the drawings attached. When the drum spins, the viewer's eye is tricked into seeing a moving image.

top tip

Some animators don't draw their characters at all. Instead they make models of them. Then they use a camera to take an image before moving the model slightly and taking another image. This is called 'stop-motion' animation and it is used in the Wallace & Gromit animations.

Cel animation

The first filmed animations appeared in the early 1900s. Each image was drawn separately and the image, or frame, was recorded with a camera. The process became faster with the invention of clear celluloid sheets, known as cels. The characters were drawn on cels and laid over a background drawing. This reduced the drawing time, because only the 'moving' characters had to be redrawn for each frame.

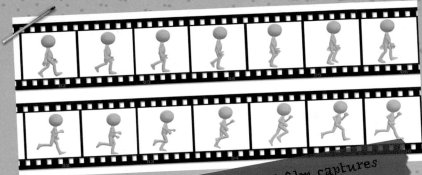

Each frame of film captures one 'moment' in the sequence of the running figure.

Flipbooks are simple to create, fun animations.

Flipping brilliant!

To make a flipbook, you'll need a small, blank notebook made with good quality paper. Draw a ball in the top right hand corner of the first page. Then, on the following pages, re-draw the ball at a slightly lower position each time. When the ball reaches the bottom of the page, make it look slightly flattened, as if it is hitting the ground. Then, on the next pages, move it up a little each time. When you flip through the pages, back to front, it will look as if the ball is falling, then bouncing.

THE EXPERT SAYS...

Nick Park, creator of Wallace and Gromit, says: *"As a child, I was always drawing comics: my dream was to work for The Beano. But when I was about 10, my dad said I could use his Super 8 camera. I started doing animations with flipbooks, and then I discovered Plasticine."*

Walt Disney

When I hear the name Walt Disney, I think of big feature-length animated cartoons like *The Lion King* or *Aladdin* with lots of action and drama. Walt Disney was also the man who created cartoon characters like Mickey Mouse and Donald Duck. He set up a world-famous animation studio that developed all kinds of new techniques and special effects.

Mickey Mouse and friends

Walt Disney started making short, silent, black and white animations in the 1920s. He set up a studio in Hollywood, California and soon introduced voices for his characters. His first major success came with Mickey Mouse, based on a pet mouse he'd once cared for. To begin with, Mickey was voiced by Disney himself! Other Disney creations such as Donald Duck and Pluto soon followed.

Walt Disney with some of his cartoon creations.

Walt Disney watches an animator at work on a scene from Pinocchio.

Disney expands

Disney didn't invent cel animation, but he was one of the first to see its potential. By the 1940s, his studio employed hundreds of animators, inkers, colourists, camera operators, voice actors, musicians, sound engineers and editors. They all had different jobs to do in the production of feature-length cartoons such as *Snow White and the Seven Dwarfs*. Nowadays Disney combines traditional cel animation techniques with computer generated imagery, or CGI.

top tip

How might one of your cartoon characters sound? For example, Mickey Mouse (centre) has quite a high, squeaky voice, while Donald Duck (right) has a quacky voice! Practise voicing the words of a cartoon character you have created. Aim for something distinctive, but easy to understand. Try recording yourself speaking in your character's voice, or get a friend to voice it for you.

The Simpsons

Matt Groening and some of the actors who provide the voices on The Simpsons pose for pictures on the Hollywood Walk of Fame with giant models of Bart and Homer.

Everyone has heard of *The Simpsons*. We all recognise the look of the characters with their yellow skin and round, bulging eyes. Their voices are really distinctive, too, and some have special catchphrases such as Homer's "Doh". I've watched loads of episodes and I feel like I know Marge, Homer, Bart, Lisa and Maggie Simpson pretty well!

Characterisation

The Simpsons is about an 'ordinary' family and is set in the fictional US city of Springfield. It pokes fun at all kinds of human behaviour, and during the three decades in which the show has been running its cast has grown to include dozens of minor characters who appear and reappear from time to time. The five Simpson family members have distinctive, recognisable traits, and they never age!

Marge and Homer Simpson with their creator, Matt Groening.

Matt Groening says that when he invented the Simpsons characters, he made "a very deliberate attempt to follow in the footsteps of Walt Disney. For instance, I made Bart like Mickey Mouse in the sense that he would always be recognisable in silhouette."

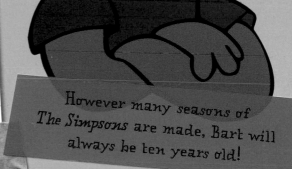

CHECKLIST

The *Simpsons* is a memorable cartoon in many ways. So, what makes your cartoon stand out? Think about:

- ☑ style of drawing
- ☑ a simple colour scheme
- ☑ stand-out characters
- ☑ catchphrases
- ☑ any common themes in each strip or episode

However many seasons of *The Simpsons* are made, Bart will always be ten years old!

Teamwork

It takes nine months to make one episode of *The Simpsons*. First, a team of 15 scriptwriters comes up with ideas and jokes, then one or two writers write a full script and actors record the voices. The animating team then draws a rough plan for each scene — a storyboard — with sketches for individual drawings, or frames. These are sent overseas to be re-drawn, inked and coloured, shot under camera, linked with voices and have the music added.

Computer animation

Many of the cartoons I watch on TV aren't hand-drawn. Instead they are designed and animated using computer graphics. In a computer-generated feature film such as *Kung Fu Panda*, the detail and special effects are amazing! The animals' fur and the ripples in the water look almost real.

Keyframing

Most animated films require between 24 and 30 separate frames per second if they are to trick the eye and make the movement look smooth and natural. That's a lot of frames! To make it easier, the animator usually programmes certain 'key frames' or key points of movement every few frames, and then lets the software calculate what happens between these key frames.

Angelina Jolie at the premiere of
Kung Fu Panda 2 in Hollywood, USA.

Motion capture

Another technique is to film live actors wearing hundreds of special markers which are picked up by video camera as they act out the scene to be animated. These movements are then applied to the animated character. This technique is called 'motion capture'. It was used to film the part of Gollum in *Lord of the Rings*.

US President Barack Obama takes part in a motion capture demonstration at the DreamWorks Animation studio in California.

You can see in this demonstration studio how the green screen behind the children is replaced (at the top of this photo) with an animated scene.

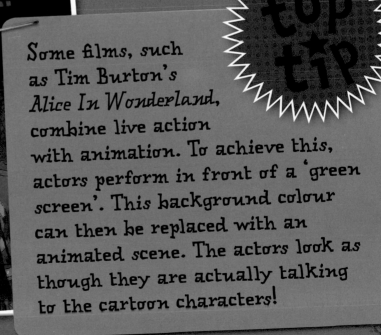

Some films, such as Tim Burton's *Alice In Wonderland*, combine live action with animation. To achieve this, actors perform in front of a 'green screen'. This background colour can then be replaced with an animated scene. The actors look as though they are actually talking to the cartoon characters!

top tip

Make your own CG animation

There are lots of free websites to get you started.

Me and my friend Ty are making our first CG animation. The character is based on my baby brother Cory. We drew several cartoon versions of him from different angles and uploaded and animated them on the computer. He crawls round a photograph background of my living room. The cartoon is called Cory's Capers. We want to make a whole series!

Choose your software

Before you start, visit some of the many free websites that help you create your own computer-generated animation. You'll need to decide how much creative freedom you want. Some sites simply allow you to select from several characters, voices and backgrounds that have been designed for you. Others allow you to upload your own drawings and add your own sound effects.

top tip To make your animation stand out, make sure you tell a story but keep it short – aim for 20 or 30 seconds to begin with. Also, try to finish with something your audience won't have seen coming – surprise them!

26

Get creative!

First you need a character. If you're designing your own, either draw one, or take a photo of a character such as a toy. Erase or delete any background and upload the image into some animation software. This will allow you to create a basic skeleton with 'joints' at points of movement. Once you have this skeleton you can manipulate your character, using the 'keyframing' technique. Then you add background and sound!

A toy such as Mike from Monsters Inc is perfect for a home-made CG animation.

CHECKLIST

To make your own computer animation you will need:

- ☑ a character
- ☑ a camera to take still images
- ☑ a computer and some animation software
- ☑ a story
- ☑ some sound effects

My cartoon world

I don't just love cartoons – I'm mad about them! I'm always reading them, watching them, talking about them, drawing them and now I'm starting to animate them. They make me laugh and I enjoy expressing myself in cartoon situations and through cartoon characters. The world wouldn't be half as much fun without them!

Comic book conventions

If you are a fan of comics, try visiting a comic book convention. You'll meet loads of like-minded people who are just as crazy about cartoons as you. At most conventions you'll see all your favourite comic stuff for sale, you might get to meet the authors and illustrators and some people even go dressed up as their favourite superhero or manga character!

A visitor 'in character' at a comic convention in New York, USA.

A black pen on white paper makes a strong image. It's also cheap to print if you want to make copies for your friends.

Start your own cartoon club

You don't have to travel to meet fellow cartoon-crazies! Why not set up a club where you can get together with your friends to share cartoons, read or make comics or collaborate on your own animations? You even could set up your own animation studio. You'll need a name, and of course an eye-catching cartoon character for your logo.

top tip

Remember, your drawings don't need to be complicated. Eyes can be dots. Legs can be sticks. Simple drawings can still tell a funny or epic story!

CHECKLIST

Here's some cartoon fun you can have with a friend.

☑ Each of you draws a stick figure.

☑ Give your stick figure one prop – a hat, a ball, a dog...

☑ Draw a speech bubble near its head.

☑ What would your stick figure say when it meets your friend's stick figure?

☑ What happens next?

Quiz

How mad about cartoons are you? Try this quiz and find out!

1. Who created *The Simpsons*? Was it:

(a) Matt Groening;

(b) Charles Montgomery Burns;

(c) Comic Book Guy?

2. What makes a superhero? Is it:

(a) wearing a special costume;

(b) keeping your identity secret;

(c) having a superpower that you use for the common good?

3. When making a film using both live action and animation, what colour screen is used behind the actors? Is it:

(a) blue;

(b) green;

(c) black?

4. What is the word for a single boxed picture in a comic strip or comic book? Is it:

(a) a frame;

(b) a panel;

(c) a portrait?

5. What is the word for 'comic' in Japanese? Is it:

(a) manga;

(b) animé;

(c) Pokémon?

6. What is the job title of the person who inks in the words in a comic book? Is it:

(a) inker;

(b) writer;

(c) letterer?

7. What kind of animation is Wallace & Gromit? Is it:

(a) motion capture;

(b) stop-motion animation;

(c) cel animation?

8. What is the most important requirement for a cartoonist? Is it:

(a) strong artistic skills;

(b) lots of pens;

(c) imagination?

Answers:
1(a), 2(c), 3(b), 4(b), 5(a), 6(c), 7(b), 8(c)

30

Glossary

animation A series of linked images, shown in rapid sequence so that the images appear to be moving.

animé Japanese animated cartoons.

caption The words that accompany a picture to complete a cartoon.

caricature A cartoon that exaggerates a real person's features.

cel A sheet of clear celluloid used in cel animation.

CGI Computer Generated Imagery.

colourist The person who adds colour to a cartoon.

comic strip A sequence of two or more separate cartoon panels that together tell a joke or a story.

flipbook A book with an image at one edge of the page that is altered a little on each separate page. When the pages are 'flipped' the image appears to move.

frame A single image in an animated cartoon.

graphic novel A book length story in comic book form.

green screen A technique to separate out live actors from the real-world scene around them, which is then replaced by a computer-generated scene or animation.

inker The person who inks in the outlines of a cartoon.

keyframing A feature of computer-generated animation where the animator programmes the key frames only and lets the computer calculate what happens between these key frames.

letterer The person who inks in the words of a cartoon.

live action The use of real actors in a film.

manga The Japanese word for comic.

motion capture A technique in which live actors are filmed wearing markers on their bodies which are then applied to an animated character to make its movements look realistic.

panel A single drawing within a cartoon strip.

penciller The person who sketches the cartoon drawings in pencil.

personality trait An individual characteristic such as laziness or smartness.

plotter The person who creates the story for a cartoon.

scriptwriter The person who writes the script for an animated cartoon.

speech bubble A shape containing the words a cartoon character speaks.

stop-motion animation The process of using models rather than drawings to make an animated film. Between each frame, the model is moved a tiny amount.

storyboard A plan with sketches for each scene of a comic book or animation.

Index